Dad, Sam, and Pat

By Sue Dickson

Illustrated by Joy Allen

MODERN CURRICULUM PRESS

Pearson Learning Group

ISBN: 0-7652-3167-0

Printed in the United States of America.

8 9 10   07

Modern
Curriculum
Press

Pearson Learning Group

1-800-321-3106
www.pearsonlearning.com

Vocabulary Words

Short ă Words

1. add
2. and
3. back
4. bag
5. can

6. cap
7. clam
8. clap
9. crab
10. Dad

11. fast
12. glad
13. had
14. hat
15. man

Vocabulary Words continued

16. map

17. nap

18. Pat

19. Pat's

20. raft

21. ran

22. sad

23. Sam

24. sand

25. sat

26. van

27. a (ŭ)

28. the (thŭ)

Pat ran.
Sam ran.

Dad had a van.

Dad had a map.

Pat had a hat.
Dad had a can.

Sam had a bag.

Dad ran fast.
Sam ran fast.

Pat ran fast.

Dad had sand.

Sam had sand.
Pat had sand.

Dad can add sand.
Sam can add sand.

Pat can add a clam.

Dad had a crab.

Dad sat.
Dad had a bag.

Dad had a cap.

Sam and Pat had a nap.

Dad! Dad!
Pat ran. Sam ran.

Sad Sam! Sad Pat!

Sad Dad!

A man had a raft.

A man had Pat's hat.

Dad ran. Sam and
Pat ran.

Pat had the hat back.

Glad Pat!